Contents

What's the weather today?

There are many different kinds of weather.

It can be hot or cold …

Weather

Claire Llewellyn

W

FRANKLIN WATTS

LONDON·SYDNEY

First published in 2005 by Franklin Watts
96 Leonard Street, London EC2A 4XD

Franklin Watts Australia
Level 17/207 Kent Street, Sydney NSW 2000

Text copyright © Claire Llewellyn 2005
Design and concept © Franklin Watts 2005

Series adviser: Gill Matthews, non-fiction literacy
*   consultant and Inset trainer*
Series editor: Rachel Cooke
Editor: Sarah Ridley
Series design: Peter Scoulding
Designer: Jemima Lumley

*Acknowledgements: Derrick Beavis/Ecoscene 13; Stephen Dalton/NHPA 18l; Alexandra Elliott Jones/Ecoscene cover,
11; Chris Fairclough title page, imprint page, 18r, 22, 23r; Peter Frischmuth/Still Pictures 10; Dan Griggs/NHPA 16;
David Hobart/Alamy 19t; Ernie Janes/NHPA 20; Richard Janulewicz/Ecoscene 9; Mike Maidment/Ecoscene 15;
David Middleton/NHPA 6-7; Stuart Rae/WWI/Still Pictures 19b; Tapani Rasanen/WWI/Still Pictures 5t; Galen
Rowell/Still Pictures 14; Silvestris Fotoservice/FLPA 8; Stock Images/Pixland/Alamy 4; Weatherstock/Still Pictures 21;
Terry Whittaker/FLPA 17b; Martin B Withers/FLPA 12; Kent Wood/Still Pictures 17t, 23l; David Woodfall/NHPA 5b.*

A CIP catalogue record for this book is available from the British Library.

ISBN: 0 7496 6369 3
Dewey decimal classification number: 551.5

Printed in Malaysia

wet or dry ...

windy or still.

What's the weather like where you are today?

It's sunny!

On sunny days, the sky is blue. The bright Sun is warm and the weather can be very hot.

▶ *When the Sun shines, the clouds are often white and fluffy.*

Never look at the Sun, even through sunglasses. It could harm your eyes.

It's windy!

Air is all around us. We cannot see or taste it but we can feel it when it moves. Moving air is called the wind.

▲ *We can see the wind moving the trees.*

◄ *People use the wind to sail boats.*

Which way is the wind blowing? Blow some bubbles into the air outside and see which way they float.

It's cloudy and wet!

On cloudy days, the sky is grey.
We often have rain.

◄ *A raincoat and boots help to keep us dry when we go out in the rain.*

▲ *Sometimes, in a rain shower, the Sun comes out and shines through raindrops. That's when we see a rainbow.*

Rain is important. It helps plants to grow. It gives water for animals to drink.

Snow and ice

When it is very cold, everything freezes. We may have snow.

▶ *Snow is slippery. We can have fun in the snow.*

Have you ever played in the snow? What was it like?

▲ On the coldest days, there is frost on the ground and water freezes into ice.

It's foggy!

Sometimes we have mist or fog.
Days like this are chilly and damp.
We cannot see very far.

◀There is often mist in the early morning.

14

A thick fog makes it hard for drivers to see the road ahead.

Fog can be very dangerous at sea. Lighthouses help sailors to stay away from the rocks.

It's stormy!

Sometimes the weather is stormy. The wind blows and it rains heavily.

▶ *Before a storm, the wind grows stronger and the sky gets dark.*

In a thunderstorm, lightning flashes across the sky.

How do you feel in a thunderstorm?

Storms bring strong winds. They can blow down trees.

The seasons

In many parts of the world, there are four seasons in the year. Each season brings changes in the weather.

▼ *In spring, we have cool, showery weather.*

▲ *We have warmer, sunnier weather in the summer.*

◄ *Autumn weather is cooler. It can be stormy.*

▼ *In winter, the weather is much colder.*

Which is your favourite season of the year? Why do you like it?

All change!

The weather is always changing. Weather forecasts tell us what the weather will be like. They help us to plan ahead.

▲ *Farmers harvest their crops before the rain arrives.*

Storms are dangerous at sea.
Sailors need to get to the shore.

Keep a weather diary for
a week and see how the
weather changes.

I know that...

1 There are many different kinds of weather.

2 On sunny days the sky is blue.

3 On windy days we feel the air moving.

4 Grey, cloudy days often bring rain.

5 On very cold days everything freezes.

6 On foggy days we cannot see clearly.

7 In thunderstorms there is lightning and thunder.

8 Each season has a different kind of weather.

9 The weather is always changing.

Index

About this book

I Know That! is designed to introduce children to the process of gathering information and using reference books, one of the key skills needed to begin more formal learning at school. For this reason, each book's structure reflects the information books children will use later in their learning career – with key information in the main text and additional facts and ideas in the captions. The panels give an opportunity for further activities, ideas or discussions. The contents page and index are helpful reference guides.

The language is carefully chosen to be accessible to children just beginning to read. Illustrations support the text but also give information in their own right; active consideration and discussion of images is another key referencing skill. The main aim of the series is to build confidence – showing children how much they already know and giving them the ability to gather new information for themselves. With this in mind, the *I know that...* section at the end of the book is a simple way for children to revisit what they already know as well as what they have learnt from reading the book.